THE POWER OF GEMSTONES

Practical Guide to Using Gemstones with Kozyrev Mirrors, Orgone Generators, and Orgonites

Mohd Faisal

M. Faisal Publications

To the Almighty God, the supreme source of knowledge and vitality, whose creation of the Earth yields jewels of great beauty and profound strength. May this effort be a modest step toward comprehending the immense forces woven into our environment while also honoring the holy mysteries of nature.

And thank you for starting this voyage, dear reader—inquisitive, receptive, and searching. As you investigate gemstones and their capacity to awaken, balance, and elevate the energies inside and around you, may this guide serve as a lighthouse. May it stimulate your research and strengthen your bond with the universe's amazing powers.

"Let us carve gems out of our stony hearts and let them light our path to love."

~ MEVLANA RUMI

CONTENTS

CONTENTS

INTRODUCTION

Gemstones have been a part of human civilization and history since the beginning. From very early prehistoric times, humans used whatever they found shiny and brightly colored to adorn themselves.

However, as humanity began to develop and gain awareness of its surroundings, it became clear that these shiny stones were not just colorful accessories but possessed various effects and powers that influenced individuals.

In modern times, the majority of people dismiss gemology as pseudoscience. Why?

Because gemology is based on eons of trial and error. It may have started with modern humans' prehistoric ancestors like Cro-Magnon, but we have evidence that ancient Mesopotamian and Sumerian civilizations used gemstones like Lapis Lazuli, Agate, Carnelian, and Turquoise as jewelry, religious artifacts, protection from evil, symbols of status and power, and in burial rituals.

The ancient Egyptians and Indian civilizations, however, took gemology to the next level. They aligned it with science and alchemy by introducing a more systematic approach, categorizing different gems based on their effects on the human mind, body, and appearance, and linking them to celestial bodies.

For example, the pearl has a satin-white appearance, comes from water, and feels cool to the eye and touch. Thus, it is associated with the moon in Egyptian, Indian, and many other ancient cultures and civilizations.

Coincidence? I think not.

Similarly, the ruby, with its warm red color, is associated with the sun because it resembles the setting sun.

Now, you may be wondering about the concept or theory behind this classification. Let me share the secret doctrine that forms the basis of gemology and natural medicine:

> *"Similar-looking things share similar characteristics and have similar effects on parts of the human body that resemble them."*

For example, the ruby's warm, bright red color is associated with the sun.

But can you guess which of the 12 systems of the human body the ruby represents?

Yes, you're right!

The ruby is associated with the cardiovascular and circulatory systems because it resembles blood, which shares its color.

You might think, "Oh, come on, this is just a coincidence."

But let me give you another example: Yellow Sapphire is associated with the gallbladder and liver because they handle bile, which is yellow. It's also linked to adipose or fat tissues due to its yellow-brownish color.

Another example: Pearl is known for its satin-white color. Guess which parts of the body are also white? The skeletal system and the brain.

Therefore, powdered pearl has been used in natural healthcare systems such as Unani, Traditional Chinese Medicine, and Ayurveda to treat illnesses related to bones and the brain.

This can't all be a coincidence! I could give you dozens more examples. This doctrine isn't limited to gemstones but applies to food as well.

For example, milk is white and strengthens bones. Walnuts resemble the brain and are proven to be beneficial for brain health due to their high content of alpha-linolenic acid, a plant-based omega-3 fatty acid.

Red foods like pomegranate, beetroot, and tomatoes are known for their beneficial effects on blood circulation and heart health.

You may think I've cherry-picked these examples, but I encourage you to keep an open mind. Look around and see how foods and their appearance often correlate with the organs they benefit. You'll be surprised!

Besides its spicy curries, the Taj Mahal, and creative Bollywood dance moves, India is known for its rich culture and one of the oldest living civilizations. In India, there's a whole scientific medical system known as Ayurveda, based on the doctrine mentioned above. If you're interested in learning more about how it works, you can check out my previously published book on Ayurveda, *"Embracing Ayurveda: A Holistic Approach to Ageless Living."*

If you're a fan of shonen anime like *Naruto*, you might be familiar with the term "Chakra." It's not a Japanese term but comes from Sanskrit, one of the oldest languages in the world. In Sanskrit, chakra literally means "The Wheel."

Chakras are hypothetical spinning points along the spine that regulate every system in the body, such as the circulatory and nervous systems.

The chakra system extends beyond the physical body, influencing the celestial, spiritual, and astral bodies. While this book focuses on gemstones, we'll briefly touch upon the chakra system.

In this book, we will discuss all seven primary chakras in detail and the five secondary chakras in brief. You'll learn what they are, how they affect your life, what you can do to activate them, and most importantly, which gemstones can help you balance and harness the power of your chakras.

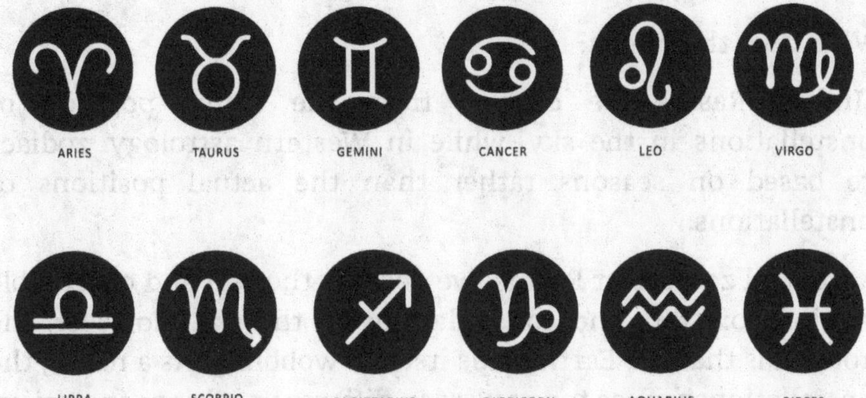

CHAPTER 1:
ZODIAC SIGNS AND GEMSTONES:

Whether we believe in it or not, most of us know what our zodiac sign is, and we often wear jewelry related to our zodiac signs. Some of us even have an interest in horoscopes and astrology.

Not only Western astrology but also other famous types, such as Indian and Chinese astrology, use zodiac signs as the basis of their systems. In Indian astrology (or Jyotish Vigyan), zodiacs are called Rashis, while in Chinese astrology, they are known as sheng xiao. Though they might seem very similar at first glance, despite sharing many similarities, they have stark differences, which we will discuss in detail.

In this book, we are going to focus on the Rashis and zodiacs in Western and Indian astrology. This is not only due to the author's expertise in these subjects compared to Chinese astrology but also because Indian astrology is based on sidereal astrology, whereas

Western astrology uses tropical astrology.

 What does that mean?

Indian Rashis are derived from the actual position of constellations in the sky, while in Western astrology, zodiacs are based on seasons rather than the actual positions of constellations.

In sidereal zodiacs or Rashis, we observe the real and observable positions of stars and constellations in the sky. However, the problem is that the Earth's axis itself is wobbling. As a result, the constellations we see today were in different positions in ancient times.

Take the equinox, for example:

The Great Pyramid of Giza was built in alignment with the star Thuban in the constellation Draco, which was the North Star 4,500 years ago. Now, Polaris has replaced Thuban as the North Star.

So, don't you think this must be taken into account when calculating zodiacs?

 Unfortunately, Western astrology fails to do so. I am not against any method, but I prefer a more accurate method of calculation, which is a rational decision rather than a biased approach.

In England, the well-known Stonehenge monument was constructed to coincide with the equinoxes and solstices. Even though these yearly occurrences still take place, the Earth's precession has caused a slight deviation in the precise alignment.

 Though gradual, this shift illustrates how the Earth's orientation in relation to the stars and constellations has changed over time.

In this book, you will find a complete chart and methods to determine your scientifically accurate zodiac sign, and only then should you wear gemstones that suit your zodiac or Rashi.

Now, let's discuss why the Western tropical zodiac is less scientific. The main criticism of tropical astrology is that it does not account for the wobbling of the Earth's axis and considers the equinoxes as fixed points, which we now know is incorrect, thanks to modern astronomical discoveries.

Tropical astrology should be treated more as a symbolic representation of the zodiacs, aligned with the Earth's seasonal patterns rather than the actual stars and constellations.

Calculating Sidereal Zodiac Sign (Rashi) From Tropical Zodiac Sign:

Since, you would most probably know your western zodiac sign. It would be easy to provide calculation system so you can yourself calculte your sidereal zodiac sign without relignying on any external or online zodiaac sign calcultors.

I will try to keepm it as simple as possible because it wont be fun if you have to do lots of maths just for finding your zodiac sign.

I would also provide complete comparison chart of both zodiac styles so you can find your sidereal by just looking at chart.

To calculte the Tropical Zodiac:

Using a date of birth, get the degree and sign of the tropical zodiac by doing the following:

1. Find the Date-Based Tropical Zodiac Sign

Every tropical zodiac sign has a corresponding set of dates. A brief reference is as follows:

	Constellation	Date Range (Tropical)
1	Aries	March 21 – April 19

2	Taurus	April 20 – May 20
3	Gemini	May 21 – June 21
4	Cancer	June 22 – July 22
5	Leo	July 23 – August 23
6	Virgo	August 24 – September 22
7	Libra	September 23 – October 23
8	Scorpio	October 24 – November 22
9	Sagittarius	November 23 – December 22
10	Capricorn	December 23 – January 20
11	Aquarius	January 21 – February 18
12	Pisces	February 19 – March 20

You can use the aforementioned ranges to find your tropical zodiac sign if you know your birthdate.

2. Determine the Degree

Using your birthdate to determine your zodiac sign, the next step is to determine the sign's degree.

Every sign of the zodiac is 30 degrees long. This is how to figure out the degree:

Degree Calculation Formula (1):

Degree= Total Days in the Sign/Days Passed in the Sign ×30

Days Passed in the Sign: This indicates the number of days that have passed since the beginning of the zodiac sign in which you were born.

Total Days in the Sign: Usually 30 or 31 days, this is the number of days in that sign.

For example suppose you were born on August 5

Then from chart you can easily find that your Tropical Zodiac sign is Leo. Since, Leo is the zodiac sign for July 23–August 23.

Now for degree, we have to calculate days Passed in the Sign.

From July 23 to August 5, total 13 days passed.

Calculation= (31-23+5)=13 days

From the chart we also know that total Days in Leo are 31 days.

Hence, on applying this data to formula (1):

Degree = 13/31*30 = 12.58°

Thus, the degree of the Sun in the tropical zodiac would be **12.58° Leo**.

To Convert A Tropical Zodiac Sign To The Sidereal Rashi:

Find the Tropical Sign:

Determine the tropical zodiac sign and degree. For above case, Tropical zodiac sign is 12.58° Leo.

Subtract the Ayanamsa:

Current Ayanamsa (2024) ≈ 23°.26' or 24°.

Example: 12.58° Leo -24°= -11.42° Leo.

Adjust if Negative:

If the result is negative, move back to the previous sign and subtract negative value from 30 or 31 (based on previous sign)

Hence, Sidereal Zodiac Rashi=(31-11.42)= 19.58° Cancer (sidereal).

Use Chart To Find Sidereal Zodiac Rashi Sign:

You can also use conversion chart to find your sidereal zodiac sign if you know you tropical Zodiac sign:

	Constellation	Tropical Date	Sidereal Date (Cyril Fagan)
1	Aries	March 21 – April 19	April 15 – May 15
2	Taurus	April 20 – May 20	May 16 – June 15
3	Gemini	May 21 – June 21	June 16 – July 16
4	Cancer	June 22 – July 22	July 17 – August 16
5	Leo	July 23 – August 23	August 17 – September 16
6	Virgo	August 24 – September 22	September 17 – October 17
7	Libra	September 23 – October 23	October 18 – November 16
8	Scorpio	October 24 – November 22	November 17 – December 16
9	Sagittarius	November 23 – December 22	December 17 – January 15
10	Capricorn	December 23 – January 20	January 16 – February 14
11	Aquarius	January 21 – February 18	February 15 – March 15
12	Pisces	February 19 – March 20	March 16 – April 14

Now, if we have to find the sidereal zodiac sign from Tropical Zodiac sign for August 5.

The Chart shows that Tropical Sign is Leo and Sidereal is Cancer.

Quick Chart:

The Gemstones And Lucky Numbers For Each Sidereal Zodiac Rashi Sign:

Zodiac	Ruling Planet	Associated Gemstone
Aquarius	Saturn	Blue Sapphire (Neelam)
Pisces	Jupiter	Yellow Sapphire (Pukhraj)
Aries	Mars	Red Coral (Moonga)
Taurus	Venus	Opal
Gemini	Mercury	Emerald (Panna)
Cancer	Moon	Pearl (Moti)
Leo	Sun	Ruby (Manik)
Virgo	Mercury	Emerald (Panna)
Libra	Venus	Opal
Scorpio	Mars	Red Coral (Moonga)
Sagittarius	Jupiter	Yellow Sapphire (Pukhraj)
Capricorn	Saturn	Blue Sapphire (Neelam)

CHAPTER 2: ASTROLOGICAL HOUSES

In sidereal astrology, every human has a 360° birth chart, and this birth chart is divided into 12 houses or blocks, each having 30°. These houses cover different aspects of a person's life and show certain elements that may affect their journey.

Note: Don't confuse the houses with the zodiac wheels because, unlike a zodiac wheel, each house is associated with a different rashi or sidereal zodiac sign.

1St House (♈)

(Motto: Vita)

The House of Self (Belongs to Aries)

It represents your appearance, personality, health, and ego.

Body Parts: Head, face, brain.

2Nd House (♉)

(Motto: Lucrum)

The House of Possessions (Belongs to Taurus):

It relates to your finances, material belongings, and voice.

Body Parts: Teeth, mouth, eyes.

3Rd House (♊)

(Motto: Fratres)

The House of Communication (Belongs to Gemini):

It governs communication, learning, siblings, and mental intelligence.

Body Parts: Hands, arms, lungs.

4Th House (♋)

(Motto: Genitor)

The House of Home (Belongs to Cancer):

It rules family, roots, real estate, and relationships, especially with your mother.

Body Parts: Chest, stomach, lungs.

5Th House (♌)

(Motto: Nati)

The House of Creativity (Belongs to Leo):

It covers creativity, romance, children, and joy.

Body Parts: Heart, spine, stomach.

6Th House (♍)

(Motto: Valetudo)

The House of Health (Belongs to Virgo):

It focuses on daily routines, health, work, and overcoming challenges.

Body Parts: Intestines, digestive system.

7Th House (♎)

(Motto: Uxor)

The House of Relationships (Belongs to Libra):

It deals with partnerships, marriage, and business alliances.

Body Parts: Lower back, kidneys.

8Th House (♏)

(Motto: Mors)

The House of Transformation (Belongs to Scorpio):

It rules over life changes, death, inheritance, and transformation.

Body Parts: Reproductive organs, pelvis.

9Th House (♐)

(Motto: Iter)

The House of Higher Learning (Belongs to Sagittarius):

It governs spirituality, travel, education, and luck.

Body Parts: Thighs, hips.

10Th House (♑)

(Motto: Regnum)

The House of Career (Belongs to Capricorn):

It focuses on career, reputation, and social status.

Body Parts: Knees, bones, joints.

11Th House (♒)

(Motto: Benefacta)

The House of Gains (Belongs to Aquarius):

It covers friendships, social circles, and long-term goals.

Body Parts: Ankles, legs.

12Th House (♓)

(Motto: Carcer)

The House of Endings (Belongs to Pisces):

It represents spirituality, isolation, subconscious mind, and closure.

Body Parts: Feet, lymphatic system.

CHAPTER 3: TYPES OF STONES FOR EACH ZODIAC SIGN OR RASHI

There are three types of stones assigned to each Sidereal Zodiac (Rashi) sign. In the next chapter, you will find all three types of gemstones: life stone, luck stone, and fortune stone. You will also find the correct size and weight of each gemstone, along with instructions on when and on which finger to wear them.

I know you might be wondering how that even works, since gemstones are solid and inert, so how can they affect human lives by influencing so-called cosmic life energy?

But remember, astrology and astronomy are two different things.

Astrology is mostly based on theories that have emerged through thousands of years of experience, trial, and error. On the other hand, astronomy is a science based on rigorous observation, experimentation, and evidence. Astrology is subjective, whereas astronomy is objective most of the time.

In more accepted terms, we can say there is a stronger correlation between a specific stone and certain zodiac signs compared to others.

Through centuries of experience, ancient cultures like those of India and China developed a system that seems highly accurate. Now, let's explore what life, luck, and destiny stones really mean.

Life Stone:

You might be wondering what the heck a life stone is. It sounds like one of the stones from Thanos' gauntlet. But aside from its fancy name, a life stone is a gemstone that is believed to be aligned with the ruling planet of your Ascendant (Sanskrit: Lagna).

In astrology, it is believed to be very beneficial, helping to attract joy, abundance, and success when worn consistently. It also promotes overall wellness and peace.

Luck Stone

Whether you believe in it or not, you have likely experienced some desirable and undesirable events purely due to luck, be it good or bad.

But what does luck really mean, and how is it different from fortune, for which you may need a different stone?

According to the Oxford Dictionary, luck is a pleasant event or fortunate incident that happens by sheer chance.

It can be good or bad, but one thing is always present: the unexpected timing of its occurrence. In simple terms, luck is any event that happens to you randomly, bringing either a positive or negative outcome.

The main difference between luck and fortune is that luck is random, unexpected, and short-term, whereas fortune is larger in scope, long-term, and often planned. Thus, for both luck and fortune, different stones are required, each associated with different celestial bodies.

Fortune stone

At first glance, a fortune stone may seem very similar to a luck stone, but there is a major difference in their purpose and effects.

Unlike a luck stone, which provides temporary, unexpected gains, a fortune stone brings destiny-driven, long-term prosperity and helps the wearer align their life with a greater purpose.

The fortune stone is believed to work based on the planet governing the ninth house of the person. It also helps individuals tackle and overcome obstacles that stand in the way of their long-term success.

CHAPTER 4:
GEMSTONES FOR
EACH ZODIAC SIGN:

Gemstones For Aries

For Poeple With DOB (From April 15 to May 15)

Aries are very lucky because they have some of the most beautiful gemstones associated with thier Rashi or Sidereal zodiac.

In This chapter we will discuss LIfe stone, Lucky stone, and Destiny stone. You will also learn ideal size for these stones and when you should wear them and also some precautions and tips.

Life Stone (Red Coral):

A luck stone is believed to bring unexpected good opportunities and events into your life, which may not only help in your personal or professional life but could also change the course of your entire life for the better.

Whether you call it a placebo or a positive morale booster, many users have reported the luck stone to be highly effective.

Ruling planet of Aries is Mars.

Thus, **life stone aligned with Mars**.

For Aries, the life stone is Red Coral.

Ideal Weight of Gesmtone:

You are allowed to wear 3 to 16 Carats of Red Coral Gemstone. Keep in mind that any gemstone above or below given range would be effective to the point that there is no point of wearing it besides fashio or asrthetic purposes.

How To Wear:

You should always wear Red Coral on your ring finger and the base metal must be any precious inert metal such as gold, silver or platinum.

Effects of Gemstone Inside Kozyrev Mirror:

Red Coral, associated with Mars, may boost focus and courage, resulting in a greater connection during mirror sessions. The partnership with Mars might boost confidence and eliminate distractions, allowing use to receive more detailed and directed information.

Luck Stone (Ruby):

For Aries, the luck stone is Ruby.

Ideal Weight of Gemstone:

You should wear a Ruby weighing **2 carats**. Any gemstone above or below this value may have little to no effect beyond fashion or aesthetic purposes.

How To Wear:

Ruby should always be worn on the **ring finger**, with the base metal being Gold.

As a luck stone for Aries, Ruby aligns with the celestial body that governs the ninth house of the Aries sign. According to ancient astrological scriptures like the "Bhrigu Samhita (600–400 B.C.E.)" and the "Brihat Parashara Hora Shastra (700–800 C.E.)", the luck stone works by aligning your efforts with fate through karma.

This alignment helps bring good luck when it's most needed, in the most unexpected ways. It also removes obstacles, paving the way for both personal and professional growth and success.

Fortune Stone (Yellow Sapphire)

For Aries, the luck stone is Yellow Sapphire (Pukhraj)

Ideal Weight of Gemstone:

You should wear a Ruby weighing **2 carats**. Any gemstone above or below this value may have little to no effect beyond fashion or aesthetic purposes.

How to Wear:

Ruby should always be worn on the **index finger**, with the base metal being Gold.

Gemstones For Taurus

For Poeple With DOB (From May 16 to June 16)

Life Stone (Diamond):

More than just a jewel, a life stone is thought to bolster your ruling planet, which for Taurus is Venus. Wearing your life stone can help you overcome challenges and attract riches, success, and pleasure. Through its cosmic rays, this stone affects every aspect of your being and is thought to be vital for general wellbeing.

For Taurus, the luck stone is Diamond

It is aligned with the ruling planet Venus.

Diamond resembles extremely bright planet Venus and share some of its nature with Astrological Planet Venus.

(Keep in mind we are not talking about astronomical planet venus.

Ideal Weight of Gemstone:

The optimal weight is 1 carat.

How to Wear:

The diamond, which can be set in silver or gold, should be worn on your middle finger.

Effects of Gemstone Inside Kozyrev Mirror:

Diamonds, which represent Venus, are believed to promote tranquility and mental clarity. They might aid in mental relaxation during Kozyrev mirror sessions, which would make it easier and more stable for users to receive information.

Lucky Stone (Ruby)

Wearing a lucky diamond for Taurus can bring positive surprises and unanticipated chances, ensuring the wheel of luck is turning in your favor.

For Aries, the luck stone is Ruby. The gemstone emerald (Panna)

Ideal Weight of Gemstone:

The optimal weight is 1.5 carats.

How to Wear:

Wear your emerald in the little or ring finger; gold is the metal of choice.

Fortune Stone (Blue Sapphire)

The planet that rules your ninth house is connected to your Fortune Stone, also called the Bhagya Stone. For Taurus, this indicates significant long-term prosperity and connection with your destiny. This stone brings you long-term success in both your personal and professional life by assisting you in overcoming barriers to achievement.

For Taurus, the luck stone is Blue sapphire.

Ideal Weight of Gemstone:

The optimal weight is 2 carats.

How to Wear:

For optimal effects, wear a blue sapphire set in gold on the middle finger.

Gemstones For Gemini

For Poeple With DOB (From June 16 to July 16)

Lifestone (Emerald):

For Gemini, the life stone is Emerald

It is aligned with the ruling planet Mercury.

Ideal Weight of Gemstone:

The optimal weight is 1.5 carats.

How to Wear:

For optimal effects, wear a Emerald set in gold on the ring or little finger.

Effects of Gemstone Inside Kozyrev Mirror:

Emeralds, when aligned with Mercury, can improve communication and mental sharpness. This influence may assist users in more effectively interpreting insights received from Kozyrev sessions, as well as improving perceptual accuracy.

Luck Stone (Diamond)

For Gemini, the lucky stone is Diamond

Ideal Weight of Gemstone:

The optimal weight is 1 Carat.

How to Wear:

For best results, wear a Diamond set in gold or silver on the middle finger.

Bhagya Stone (Blue Sapphire)

For Gemini, the fortune stone is Blue Sapphire.

It helps unlock hidden potential and attracts good fortune.

Ideal Weight of Gemstone:

The optimal weight is 2 Carats.

How to Wear:

For optimal benefits, wear a Blue Sapphire set in gold on the middle finger.

Gemstones For Cancer

For Poeple With DOB (From July 17 to August 16)

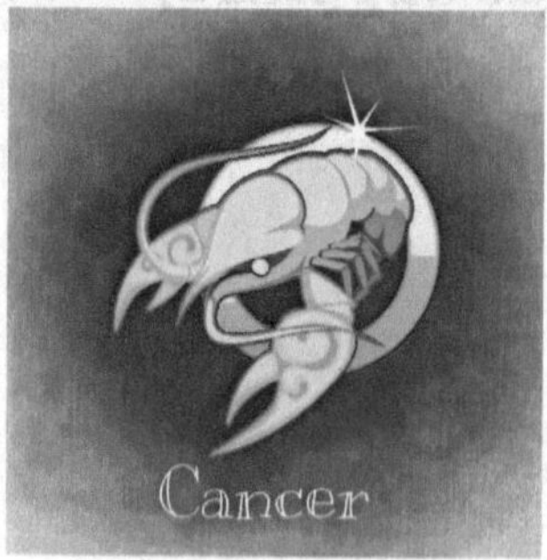

Life Stone (Pearl)

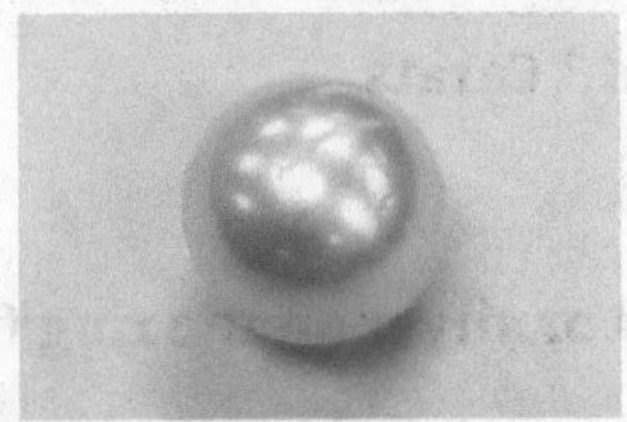

For Cancer, the life stone is Pearl

It strengthens the influence of the Moon, enhancing intuition and emotions.

Ideal Weight of Gemstone:

The optimal weight is 2 Carats.

How to Wear:

For best effects, wear a Pearl set in silver on the ring or little finger.

Effects of Gemstone Inside Kozyrev Mirror:

Pearl, being aligned with the Moon, improves intuition and emotional equilibrium. Wearing a Pearl during Kozyrev sessions may promote a more responsive and intuitive mood, resulting in a smoother flow of impressions and insights.

Luck Stone (Coral)

For Cancer, the lucky stone is Coral.

It brings courage and boosts confidence in decision-making.

Ideal Weight of Gemstone:

The optimal weight is 3 Carats.

How to Wear:

Wear Coral set in gold or silver on the ring finger.

Bhagya Stone (Yellow Sapphire)

For Cancer, the fortune stone is Yellow Sapphire

It brings fortune and success, especially in professional life.

Ideal Weight of Gemstone:

The optimal weight is 2 Carats.

How to Wear:

Wear Yellow Sapphire in gold on the index finger.

Gemstones For Leo

For Poeple With DOB (From 17 August to September 16)

Life Stone (Ruby)

For Leo, the life stone is Ruby

It strengthens the Sun's influence, bringing vitality and confidence.

Ideal Weight of Gemstone:

The optimal weight is 2 Carats.

How to Wear:

Wear a Ruby set in gold on the ring finger for optimal results.

Effects of Gemstone Inside Kozyrev Mirror:

Ruby is in harmony with the Sun, which encourages vigor and inner strength. The connection to the global field might be strengthened during sessions as Ruby's energy could boost confidence and allow users to see more deeply.

Luck Stone (Yellow Sapphire)

For Leo, the lucky stone is Yellow Sapphire

It ensures success and opens new avenues in personal and professional life.

Ideal Weight of Gemstone:

The optimal weight is 2 Carats.

How to Wear:

For best effects, wear Yellow Sapphire in gold on the index finger.

Bhagya Stone (Coral)

For Leo, the fortune stone is Coral

It helps overcome obstacles and brings good fortune when you need it the most.

Ideal Weight of Gemstone:

The optimal weight is 3 Carats.

How to Wear:

Wear Coral set in gold or silver on the ring finger.

Gemstones For Virgo

For Poeple With DOB (From September 17 to October17)

Life Stone (Emerald)

For Virgo, the life stone is Emerald

It enhances communication and intellect, strengthening

Mercury's influence.

Ideal Weight of Gemstone:

The optimal weight is 1.5 Carats.

How to Wear:

Wear an Emerald set in gold on the ring or little finger.

Effects of Gemstone Inside Kozyrev Mirror:

With Mercury as the ruling planet, Emerald improves communication and analytical abilities. This could facilitate better understanding by assisting users in processing the experience and efficiently communicating impressions in Kozyrev mirror work.

Luck Stone (Blue Sapphire)

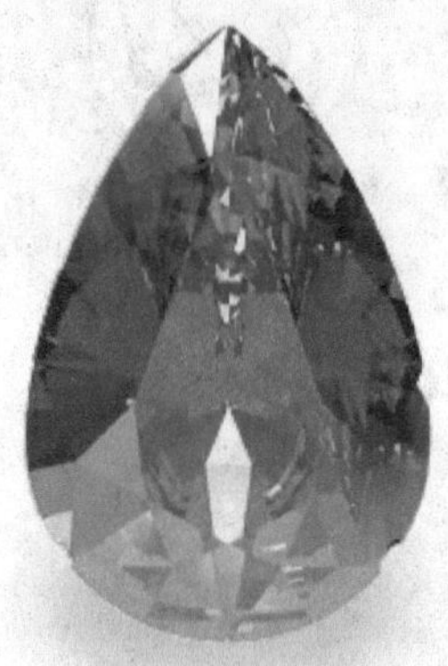

For Virgo, the lucky stone is Blue Sapphire

It brings discipline and structure, helping achieve long-term goals.

Ideal Weight of Gemstone:

The optimal weight is 2 Carats.

How to Wear:

For best results, wear Blue Sapphire in gold on the middle finger.

Bhagya Stone (Diamond)

For Virgo, the fortune stone is Diamond

It brings charm and luxury, ensuring success in all ventures.

Ideal Weight of Gemstone:

The optimal weight is 1 Carat.

How to Wear:

Wear a Diamond in gold or silver on the middle finger.

Gemstones For Libra

For Poeple With DOB (From October 18 to November 16)

Life Stone (Diamond)

For Libra, the life stone is Diamond

It brings balance and harmony, enhancing Venus's influence.

Ideal Weight of Gemstone:

The optimal weight is 1 Carat.

How to Wear:

Wear a Diamond set in gold or silver on the middle finger.

Luck Stone (Blue Sapphire):

For Libra, the lucky stone is Blue Sapphire

It enhances Saturn's influence, bringing stability and responsibility.

Ideal Weight of Gemstone:

The optimal weight is 2 Carats.

How to Wear:

Wear Blue Sapphire in gold on the middle finger for best results.

Effects of Gemstone Inside Kozyrev Mirror:

As previously said, Diamond's alignment with Venus promotes balance and harmony. Users may find it simpler to access the effects of the Kozyrev mirror and understand insights without mental distraction if they are in a centered state, which is facilitated by its calming and grounding affect.

Bhagya Stone (Emerald)

For Libra, the fortune stone is Emerald

It boosts creativity and ensures success in personal endeavors.

Ideal Weight of Gemstone:

The optimal weight is 1.5 Carats.

How to Wear:

Wear an Emerald set in gold on the ring or little finger.

Gemstones For Scorpio

For Poeple With DOB (From November 17 to December16)

Life Stone (Coral)

For Scorpio, the life stone is Coral

It enhances Mars's influence, bringing courage and determination.

Ideal Weight of Gemstone:

The optimal weight is 3 Carats.

How to Wear:

Wear Coral set in gold or silver on the ring finger.

Effects of Gemstone Inside Kozyrev Mirror:

Mars-influenced coral encourages emotional depth and resiliency. It can assist users in exploring unconscious parts of their minds during sessions, increasing their openness to the profound revelations the mirror might provide.

Luck Stone (Yellow Sapphire)

For Scorpio, the lucky stone is Yellow Sapphire

It brings wisdom and good fortune in professional life.

Ideal Weight of Gemstone:

The optimal weight is 2 Carats.

How to Wear:

Wear Yellow Sapphire in gold on the index finger.

Bhagya Stone (Pearl)

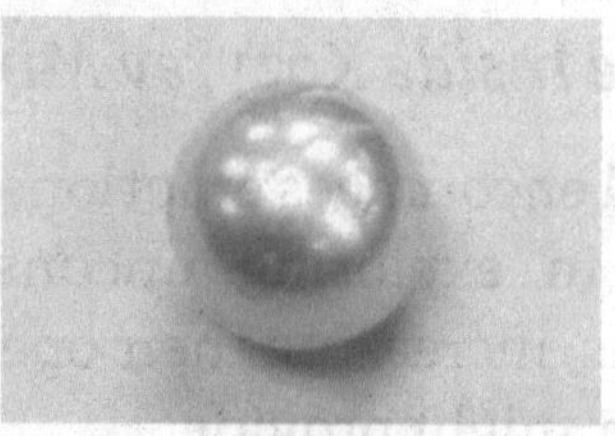

For Scorpio, the fortune stone is Pearl

It brings emotional balance and helps overcome obstacles.

Ideal Weight of Gemstone:

The optimal weight is 2 Carats.

How to Wear:

Wear Pearl set in silver on the ring finger.

Gemstones For Sagittarius

For Poeple With DOB (From December 17 to January 15)

Life Stone (Yellow Sapphire)

For Sagittarius, the life stone is Yellow Sapphire

It enhances Jupiter's influence, bringing wisdom and prosperity.

Ideal Weight of Gemstone:

The optimal weight is 2 Carats.

How to Wear:

Wear Yellow Sapphire in gold on the index finger.

Effects of Gemstone Inside Kozyrev Mirror:

Jupiter is represented by the yellow sapphire, which is associated with wisdom and spiritual development. It might enable users to access more extensive knowledge domains and insights, potentially deepening the spiritual components of a Kozyrev mirror experience.

Luck Stone (Coral)

For Sagittarius, the lucky stone is Coral

It boosts energy and confidence in personal and professional endeavors.

Ideal Weight of Gemstone:

The optimal weight is 3 Carats.

How to Wear:

Wear Coral in gold or silver on the ring finger.

Bhagya Stone (Ruby):

For Sagittarius, the fortune stone is Ruby

It brings success in leadership and business ventures.

Ideal Weight of Gemstone:

The optimal weight is 2 Carats.

How to Wear:

Wear Ruby in gold on the ring finger.

Gemstones For Capricorn

For Poeple With DOB (From January 16 to February 14)

Life Stone (Blue Sapphire)

For Capricorn, the life stone is Blue Sapphire

[=It strengthens Saturn's influence, bringing discipline and success.

Ideal Weight of Gemstone:

The optimal weight is 2 Carats.

How to Wear:

Wear Blue Sapphire set in gold on the middle finger.

Effects of Gemstone Inside Kozyrev Mirror:

Blue Sapphire, which is ruled by Saturn, can help you focus and discipline yourself. This grounding stone may help users maintain clarity during sessions and approach the experience with greater attention, thereby reducing mental distractions.

Luck Stone (Emerald):

For Capricorn, the lucky stone is Emerald

It enhances intellect and brings clarity in decision-making.

Ideal Weight of Gemstone:

The optimal weight is 1.5 Carats.

How to Wear:

Wear Emerald in gold on the ring or little finger.

Bhagya Stone (Diamond)

For Capricorn, the fortune stone is Diamond

It attracts luxury and helps achieve success in ventures.

Ideal Weight of Gemstone:

The optimal weight is 1 Carat.

How to Wear:

Wear Diamond in gold or silver on the middle finger.

Gemstones For Aquarius

For Poeple With DOB (From February 15 to March 15)

Life Stone (Blue Sapphire)

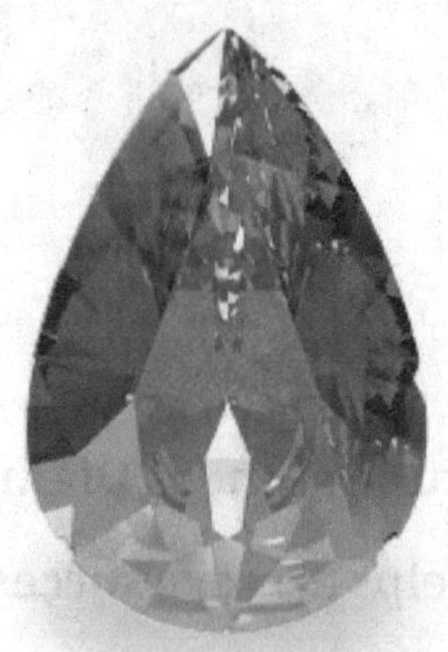

For Aquarius, the life stone is Blue Sapphire

It boosts creativity and brings discipline in life.

Ideal Weight of Gemstone:

The optimal weight is 2 Carats.

How to Wear:

Wear Blue Sapphire in gold on the middle finger.

Effects of Gemstone Inside Kozyrev Mirror:

Also aligned with Saturn, Blue Sapphire provides a calming effect that promotes thoughtful introspection. This clarity could be valuable during sessions, helping users sift through impressions with greater discernment.

Luck Stone (Emerald)

For Aquarius, the lucky stone is Emerald

It sharpens intellect and helps in communication.

Ideal Weight of Gemstone:

The optimal weight is 1.5 Carats.

How to Wear:

Wear Emerald in gold on the ring or little finger.

Bhagya Stone (Diamond)

For Aquarius, the fortune stone is Diamond

It attracts wealth and enhances social status.

Ideal Weight of Gemstone:

The optimal weight is 1 Carat.

How to Wear:

Wear Diamond set in gold or silver on the middle finger.

Gemstones For Pisces

For Poeple With DOB (From March 16 to April 14)

Life Stone (Yellow Sapphire)

For Pisces, the life stone is Yellow Sapphire

It enhances Jupiter's influence, bringing wisdom and wealth.

Ideal Weight of Gemstone:

The optimal weight is 2 Carats.

How to Wear:

Wear Yellow Sapphire set in gold on the index finger.

Effects of Gemstone Inside Kozyrev Mirror:

Yellow Sapphire, which is ruled by Jupiter, improves intuition and understanding. This influence may enhance the depth of perception during Kozyrev sessions, allowing for a more thorough connection to the information field.

Luck Stone (Pearl)

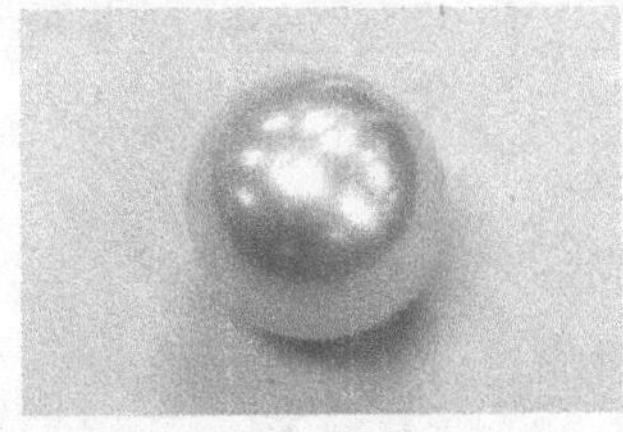

For Pisces, the lucky stone is Pearl

It promotes emotional balance and helps overcome obstacles.

Ideal Weight of Gemstone:

The optimal weight is 2 Carats.

How to Wear:

Wear Pearl set in silver on the ring finger.

Bhagya Stone (Ruby)

For Pisces, the fortune stone is Ruby

It brings vitality and success in business ventures.

Ideal Weight of Gemstone:

The optimal weight is 2 Carats.

How to Wear:

Wear Ruby set in gold on the ring finger.

CHAPTER 5:
NAVRATNI RING:

Deeply ingrained in the ancient traditions of Vedic astrology, the Navratna ring, often known as the "nine-gem" ring, represents a close bond between human existence and the universe.

It's like thanos guntlet for astrology but in a ring form.

Made with nine distinct gemstones, the ring symbolizes the nine celestial influencers in Hindu astrology: the Sun, Moon, Mars, Mercury, Jupiter, Venus, Saturn, Rahu (the north lunar node), Ketu (the south lunar node), and pearl, coral, emerald, yellow sapphire, diamond, blue sapphire, hessonite, and cat's eye.

Every stone is hand-picked for its mystical qualities and unique connection to a planetary energy, which is thought to channel positive vibrations from these celestial bodies to improve the wearer's protection, wealth, balance, and health.

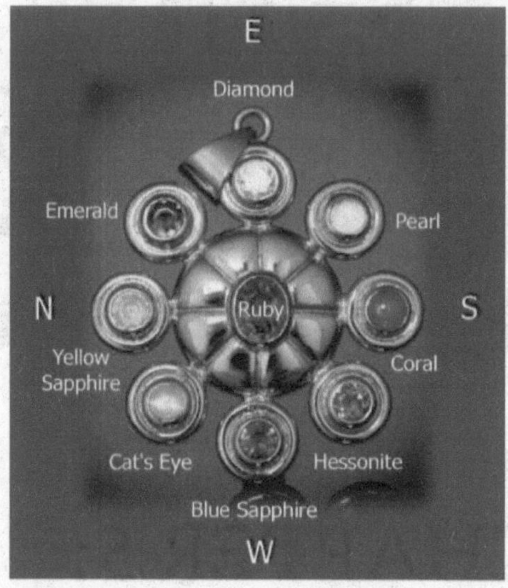

The Navratna ring was regarded as a potent talisman in ancient India, where it was thought to harmonize one's own energy with the universe, protect against unfavorable planetary influences, and amplify positive benefits.

In addition to their defensive qualities, Navratna rings were worn by kings and emperors as prestige, luck, and spirituality markers. As the Navratna tradition expanded, its impact extended to nearby areas outside of India. The Navratna acquired a home in royal jewelry in Thailand and Cambodia, where it was worn by kings to symbolize their heavenly right to reign and their responsibility to uphold cosmic order.

The Navratna ring is still in style today for people looking to align with planetary forces, gain spiritual insight, and maintain emotional equilibrium. Many individuals think that by utilizing the distinct energy of each gem, wearing a Navratna ring can enhance their well-being and sharpen their intuition.

When combined with equipment such as Kozyrev mirrors, orgonite pyramids, and energy generators, the Navratna ring is believed to promote mental clarity and increase sensitivity to subtle energies for those investigating ESP and psychic phenomena.

The ring is still a treasured representation of cosmic harmony and spiritual strength because of its historical significance and capacity to combine celestial power with individual experience.

The Navratna ring is praised for its special relationship to the celestial bodies in the ancient Vedic literature. It is said that wearing the Navratna ring aligns the wearer's life with universal harmony by channeling cosmic forces through each jewel. The Navratna stones' auspicious attributes are highlighted by a Sanskrit shloka that is frequently connected to them:

"सूर्यों रत्नं महाशक्तिं चंद्रमाणिक्यमनुत्तमम्।

गुरुरत्नं पुखराजं बुधजातमणिं तथा।

शुक्रमुक्ताहारत्नं शनिसौरस्त्र नीलकः।

राहोरत्नं गोमेदं च केतुश्च वैदूर्यकः।"

Meaning:

"The Sun bestows ruby, the Moon offers pearl, Guru (Jupiter) grants yellow sapphire, and Budh (Mercury) emerald, Venus offers diamond, Saturn, the blue sapphire, Rahu yields hessonite, and Ketu, the cat's eye."

Since each Navratna stone is associated with a particular planet and bestows its strength, balance, and protection upon its wearer, this shloka perfectly captures the spirit of the stones.

The shloka, which has its roots in ancient traditions, emphasizes that the Navratna ring serves as a channel for these celestial energies and strengthens the harmony between people and the universe.

Another Sanskrit shloka or verse, attributed to the Brihat Jataka and referenced in texts like Mani-Mala and Jataka Parijata, describes the association of nine precious gemstones with their respective planetary deities in Vedic astrology. The shloka is as follows:

माणिक्यं तरणेः सुजात्यममलं मुक्ताफलं शीतगोः

माहेयस्य च विद्रुमं मरकतं सौम्यस्य गारुत्मतम

देवेज्यस्य च पुष्पराजमसुराचार्यस्य वज्रं शनेः

नीलं निर्मलमन्ययोश्च गदिते गोमेदवैदूर्यके

Transliteration:

māṇikyaṃ taraṇeḥ sujātyamamalam muktāphalam śītagoḥ

māheyasya ca vidrumam marakatam saumyasya gārutmatama

devejyasya ca puṣparājamasurācāryasya vajram śaneḥ

nīlam nirmalamanyayośca gadite gomedavaidūryake

Explanation: The translation of this verse describes the gemstones associated with each planet in Vedic astrology as follows:

Ruby (māṇikyaṃ) for Surya (Sun), Pearl (muktāphalam) for Chandra (Moon), Red coral (vidrumam) for Mangala (Mars), Emerald (maratakam) for Budha (Mercury), Yellow sapphire (puṣparājam) for Brihaspati (Jupiter), Diamond (vajram) for Shukra (Venus), Blue sapphire (nīlam) for Shani (Saturn), Hessonite (gomeda) for Rahu (ascending lunar node), and Cat's eye (vaidūryam) for Ketu (descending lunar node). It is emphasized that "...these gemstones should be pure and flawless."

This traditional verse highlights the ancient belief that these gemstones, when high-born and free of blemishes, can strengthen one's connection to the planets and their beneficial energies.

Wearing this ring is believed to increase spiritual sensitivity, shield against bad energy, and strengthen intuition. The Navratna stones are thought to increase psychic receptivity for people exploring extrasensory perception, especially during meditation or Kozyrev mirror sessions where heightened perception is desired.

Clarity, attention, and spiritual development are fostered by the Navratna's connection with cosmic energies, which, when paired with orgonite energy generators, offers a special fusion of traditional knowledge and contemporary metaphysical techniques.

The Four Bhavas (4 Moods)

In Indian astrology, the concept of the four bhavas, or fundamental aims of life, influences the interpretation of the twelve houses (bhavas), each of which reflects a distinct aspect of human experience.

These four life goals, Dharma (duty), Artha (resources), Kama (pleasure), and Moksha (liberation), or पुरुषार्थ (Purushartha in Hindi), are the foundational pillars of a satisfying existence. The ancient sages of India thought that human life should strive for each of these goals in order to achieve harmony and balance.

1. Dharma (धर्म):

The first, fifth, and ninth houses represent Dharma, which represents one's responsibility, ethics, and moral responsibilities. It expresses the desire for meaning and to live a life that is consistent with one's values, as well as greater universal ideals.

2. *Artha* (अर्थ):

Artha appears in the second, sixth, and tenth houses, emphasizing the need for riches. This includes acquiring the resources, talents, and abilities required to support oneself and perform one's responsibilities in life, thereby laying the groundwork for stability and progress.

3. *Kama* (काम)

The 3rd, 7th, and 11th houses represent Kama, or the pursuit of pleasure, wants, and intimate relationships. It expresses our need for friendship, joy, creativity, and self-expression, and serves as a reminder of life's joys and shared experiences.

4. *Moksha* (मोक्ष)

Moksha occurs in the fourth, eighth, and twelfth houses, indicating ultimate liberation or spiritual emancipation. It is the path to inner serenity, detachment from earthly attachments, and comprehending life's greater purpose.

These four life goals occur in three cycles within the twelve houses:

Dharma (Duty) Houses	Artha (Resources) Houses	Kama (Pleasure) Houses	Moksha (Liberation) Houses
1	2	3	4
5	6	7	8
9	10	11	12

- Individual Level (1-4):

The first four houses address personal development and self-awareness.

- Relational Level (5–8):

The middle houses prioritize social connections, relationships, and emotional bonding.

- Universal Level (9-12):

The final houses focus on universal perspectives, connecting the self to higher wisdom.

This cyclical pattern reminds us of the interconnectedness of duty, affluence, desire, and liberty, urging people to live a balanced and purposeful life.

By pondering on these purusharthas, we can aim for a balanced existence that values personal development, social relationships, and spiritual fulfillment.

How To Utilize The Kozyrev Mirror's Navaratni Ring

Though the Navaratni ring is believed to be very effective for attracting good luck and fortune, its use inside the Kozyrev mirror is not well-documented or even tested. You should not believe in any assumptions and concepts that are borderline pseudoscientific.

Therefore, I urge you to test it inside the Kozyrev mirror with systematic documentation of your experience and then compare it with an experience without the ring. Here is the full plan on how you can do it:

Set a Baseline:

Start with a Kozyrev mirror session in which the Navaratni ring is not used. Keep a thorough journal of your experience, recording any shifts in consciousness, sensation, or perception.

Introduce the Navaratni Ring

Put the ring on in front of the mirror during a different session. Maintain consistency in the setup, length, and focus of the session.

Record Observations:

While wearing the ring, note any new or enhanced feelings, mental clarity, or intuitive perceptions.

Compare Sessions:

Following a few sessions, examine how the experiences with and without the Navaratni ring differ from one another. Do any impacts stand out or can they be replicated?

Draw Conclusions:

Consider how the ring affected the session, if at all. Does it feel better or worse? Make your own conclusions based on these data, and if you have any more ideas, share them.

A methodical approach is ensured by testing with documentation, which enables you to make insightful conclusions about whether the Navaratni ring actually affects your experience in the Kozyrev mirror.

Table For Kozyrev Mirror Sessions		
Metric	Session with Navaratni Ring	Session without Navaratni Ring
Blood Pressure		
Heart Rate		
Oxygen Level (SpO₂)		
Body Temperature		
Mood/Emotional State		
Subjective ESP Sensitivity		
Duration of Altered State		
Notable Experiences		

Notes:

- **BP**: Blood Pressure
- **Heart Rate**: Beats per Minute (bpm)
- **SpO2**: Oxygen Saturation in Blood
- **Body Temp**: Body Temperature in Fahrenheit
- **Mood Before/After**: Any emotional state changes before and after the session (calm, anxious, focused, etc.)

- **Mental Clarity**: Rate from 1-10, where 10 is very clear, and 1 is unfocused
- **Physical Sensations**: Note any tingling, warmth, or other bodily sensations
- **Intuition/ESP Sensitivity**: Note any significant intuitive or sensory experiences

Use this table to document each session consistently, which will help you assess any effects the Navaratni ring may have during Kozyrev mirror sessions.

For example:
Sample Session Table:

Sample Session Table:

Metric	Session with Navaratni Ring	Session without Navaratni Ring
Blood Pressure	120/80 mmHg	118/78 mmHg
Heart Rate	75 bpm	80 bpm
Oxygen Level (SpO_2)	0.98	0.97
Body Temperature	98.6°F (37°C)	98.2°F (36.8°C)
Mood/Emotional State	Calm, Focused	Slightly Anxious
Subjective ESP Sensitivity	Moderate	Low
Duration of Altered State	20 minutes	15 minutes
Notable Experiences	Tingling sensation, increased clarity	Mild relaxation

ABOUT THE AUTHOR

Mohd Faisal

Indian author and publisher Mohd Faisal is known for his extensive contributions to fiction and nonfiction literature. Initially trained in Chemical Engineering, stemming from his expertise in a variety of disciplines With over 70 published works on self-help, parenting, parapsychology, permaculture, finance, religion, and occult studies, Faisal's expertise is admired by readers worldwide.

Bestsellers like "Kozyrev Mirror & ESP" (2023), "Zener Cards & ESP" (2023), "Orgone Accumulator & ESP" (2023), "Ikigai Blueprint" (2023), "Raising ADHD Champions" (2024), "Parenting with Style" (2023), and "Alchemy Handbook" (2023) exemplify his commitment to empowering and enlightening audiences across a wide range of topics.

BOOKS IN THIS SERIES

Kozyrev Mirror Uncovered: Everything You Need to Know and Learn

Take this extensive series on an amazing voyage into the realm of Kozyrev mirrors. Each book offers a thorough examination of the science, history, and real-world uses of these potent tools, providing insight into how they could unleash human potential and provide access to different states of consciousness.

Kozyrev Mirror And Esp: Unlock Third Eye Of Esp- A Journey Into Esp And Kozyrev Mirrors

Unveiling the Cosmic Gateway: Investigate the Kozyrev Mirror and Awaken Extraordinary Powers!

With our innovative book, "The Kozyrev Mirror: A Guide to Torsion, ESP, and Beyond," embark on an incredible voyage into the regions of the unknown. Uncover the mysteries of this mysterious mirror as we dig into the enthralling world of the Kozyrev Effect, providing readers with an unprecedented grasp of torsion, awareness, and the boundless possibilities that lay inside.

Key Ideas Revealed:
Dive deep into the Kozyrev Mirror's underlying principles, discovering the mysteries of torsion fields and their significant impact on our view of reality. Gain a thorough understanding of the Kozyrev Effect and its consequences for consciousness inquiry, opening the door to a new level of comprehension.

How To Make and Use Kozyrev Mirrors:

With our step-by-step blueprints, clear instructions, and precise dimensions, you can learn how to build your own Kozyrev Mirrors. This crucial section allows readers to interact with this revolutionary technology firsthand, providing a concrete link to the esoteric world of torsion fields.

Creating Bridges Between Worlds:
Learn not only how to construct a Kozyrev Mirror, but also how to efficiently harness its power. Investigate the mirror's applications, which range from improving meditation to strengthening intuitive powers. Learn about the transforming power it has for both personal and spiritual growth.

How to Awaken ESP Powers:
Use the Kozyrev Mirror and other applications in the book to activate your latent extrasensory perception (ESP) abilities. Learn how to use the energy of the mirror to raise your consciousness, increase your intuitive abilities, and open the door to heightened awareness.

Practical Advice and Real-Life Applications:
Get practical advice on how to use the Kozyrev Mirror in your daily life. Investigate real-world applications ranging from improving remote seeing to increasing healing energies. Consider the significant influence that old knowledge can have on the current world.

The Kozyrev Mirror: Science and Spirituality:
This book smoothly links science and spirituality together, producing a tapestry that allows readers to explore undiscovered territories of awareness. "The Kozyrev Mirror" provides a roadmap to unlocking your actual potential, whether you are a seasoned practitioner or a curious beginning.

Are You Prepare to Break Through the Veil?

Set out on a self-discovery quest, unravel the mysteries of the Kozyrev Mirror, and awaken the amazing within. This book is your ticket to a realm where science meets the mystical, providing a fresh look at the interdependence of mind, matter, and the cosmos.

All About The Kozyrev Mirrors: History, Development, And Science Explained

All About The Kozyrev Mirrors: History, Development, and Science Explained is the definitive guide to solving one of science's most intriguing mysteries. Unlock the Secrets of the Kozyrev Mirrors!

This book is not just another entry in the field; it is a meticulously crafted resource that stands out because of:

- Detailed Historical Synopsis: Follow the development of Kozyrev Mirrors from their inception to their influence on current research.
- In-Depth Hypotheses Exploration: Learn the four main theories guiding Kozyrev Mirror experiments through in-depth analyses and knowledgeable commentary.
- Modern Scientific Context: Find out how modern scientific viewpoints support or refute the idea of torsion fields, offering an impartial assessment of its viability.
- In-depth Ray Propagation Studies: Analyze the different kinds of rays in the mirrors and their behavior, providing concise justifications for their importance.
- Detailed Research Review: Get access to a carefully selected overview of recent findings on torsion fields and their essential properties, presented in a way that has never been seen before.
- Unique Graphical Aids: Gain access to special illustrations, diagrams, and visual aids that clarify difficult ideas and improve comprehension.

All About The Kozyrev Mirrors offers a singular, all-encompassing viewpoint that is unavailable elsewhere by fusing scientific precision with historical depth. Ideal for scholars, learners, and enthusiasts alike, this book is your passport to delving into the remarkable possibilities of Kozyrev Mirrors.

Get your copy right away and take a trip through the cutting-edge intersection of science and history.

How To Use Kozyrev Mirror: A Kozyrev Mirror User Guide

With the Kozyrev Mirror User Manual, set out on a life-changing adventure. Your key to unlocking the deep impacts and long-forgotten mysteries of the Kozyrev Mirror is this all-inclusive guide.

What You'll Discover:
1.: Recognize the ways in which the Kozyrev Mirror modifies and amplifies the energy fields of living things.
2. Bring a comprehensive list of Arctic exploration cities, together with elevations and coordinates between 73°N and 90°N, to your sessions.
3. Practice transcendental, vipassana, and Sufi zikr meditations to develop the ability to reach and sustain elevated levels of consciousness.
4. Adhere to a regimented schedule intended to optimize your gains and experience.
5. Learn the significance of the Kozyrev Mirror and the reasons behind the deformed skull shapes of ancient nations.
6. Practices like Boat Pose, Warrior Pose, and even Laughter Yoga can help you become more aware of the world around you.
7. Utilizing yoga poses, open and harmonize all 12 chakras to awaken your energy centers.

Why This Book Is Unique
The Kozyrev Mirror User Manual explores the mirror's esoteric and scientific sides in greater detail than previous manuals. It offers a special combination of information that appeals to

both the inquisitive and the knowledgeable by fusing historical insights with useful instructions. This manual gives you the skills to change your reality and raise your consciousness, so it's more than just a guidebook—it's a voyage into the unknown.

Grab your copy right now to explore a whole new level of comprehension!

Esp Mastery: Boost Your Psychic Abilities And Awareness

Unlock the Extraordinary Within You: ESP Mastery: A Book Unlike Any Other

"ESP Mastery: Boost Your Psychic Abilities and Awareness" serves as a beacon of enlightenment in a world where curiosity knows no boundaries and the hunt for the unusual beckons. This is more than a book; it is a transforming trip into the depths of human potential.

Why Should You Choose This Book Over Others:

1. thorough Insight: "ESP Mastery" is a thorough book that delves into the intriguing world of Extra Sensory Perception (ESP). It doesn't just skim the surface; it goes deep into the subject, providing you with a comprehensive comprehension of psychic phenomena.

2. Scientific Approach: In contrast to many other works on the subject, "ESP Mastery" adopts a balanced approach, mixing old knowledge with current science. It links the magical and intellectual worlds, offering a firm platform for your investigation.

3. Practical Exercises: This book isn't only about theory; it's also about doing. You'll be able to actively develop and improve your psychic talents via a variety of hands-on activities and procedures. "ESP Mastery" is your dependable companion on your

path to self-discovery.

4. Clarity and Guidance: Written in an easy-to-understand style, this book provides guidance that even newbies to the realm of ESP may grasp. It simplifies and manages difficult topics by demystifying them.

5. New Perspectives: "ESP Mastery" offers a unique viewpoint. It mixes old wisdom with current ideas to provide a comprehensive understanding of psychic talents. Whether you're a beginner or a seasoned practitioner, you'll discover fresh ideas and techniques to try.

What new in "ESP Mastery"?

Current Research: This book incorporates the most recent findings and research in the subject of psychic phenomena, guaranteeing that you have access to the most current knowledge.

Mind Body Connection: "ESP Mastery" explores the relationship between your mind, body, and psychic skills. It delves into the transformative power of mindfulness, meditation, and holistic wellness techniques on your ESP journey.

Ethical Exploration: The book highlights ethical practices and the responsible use of your newly acquired skills. It teaches you how to handle the nuances of ESP while maintaining your integrity and respect for others.

"ESP Mastery" is your key to unlocking the remarkable within you in a world where curiosity and the desire for selfdiscovery are celebrated. This book is about personal growth, awareness, and the limitless potential of the human mind, not only psychic talents. Explore the unexplored world of your own psyche and uncover your dormant talents.

~ THE END ~